THIS TEACHER PLANNER BELONGS TO:

2022 – 2023

www.amazon.com/author/angelduran

2022

July

S	M	T	W	T	F	S
					1	2
3	4	5	6	7	8	9
10	11	12	13	14	15	16
17	18	19	20	21	22	23
24	25	26	27	28	29	30
31						

August

S	M	T	W	T	F	S
	1	2	3	4	5	6
7	8	9	10	11	12	13
14	15	16	17	18	19	20
21	22	23	24	25	26	27
28	29	30	31			

September

S	M	T	W	T	F	S
				1	2	3
4	5	6	7	8	9	10
11	12	13	14	15	16	17
18	19	20	21	22	23	24
25	26	27	28	29	30	

October

S	M	T	W	T	F	S
						1
2	3	4	5	6	7	8
9	10	11	12	13	14	15
16	17	18	19	20	21	22
23	24	25	26	27	28	29
30	31					

November

S	M	T	W	T	F	S
		1	2	3	4	5
6	7	8	9	10	11	12
13	14	15	16	17	18	19
20	21	22	23	24	25	26
27	28	29	30			

December

S	M	T	W	T	F	S
				1	2	3
4	5	6	7	8	9	10
11	12	13	14	15	16	17
18	19	20	21	22	23	24
25	26	27	28	29	30	31

Academic # 2023 School Planner

January

S	M	T	W	T	F	S
1	2	3	4	5	6	7
8	9	10	11	12	13	14
15	16	17	18	19	20	21
22	23	24	25	26	27	28
29	30	31				

February

S	M	T	W	T	F	S
			1	2	3	4
5	6	7	8	9	10	11
12	13	14	15	16	17	18
19	20	21	22	23	24	25
26	27	28				

March

S	M	T	W	T	F	S
			1	2	3	4
5	6	7	8	9	10	11
12	13	14	15	16	17	18
19	20	21	22	23	24	25
26	27	28	29	30	31	

April

S	M	T	W	T	F	S
						1
2	3	4	5	6	7	8
9	10	11	12	13	14	15
16	17	18	19	20	21	22
23	24	25	26	27	28	29
30						

May

S	M	T	W	T	F	S
	1	2	3	4	5	6
7	8	9	10	11	12	13
14	15	16	17	18	19	20
21	22	23	24	25	26	27
28	29	30	31			

June

S	M	T	W	T	F	S
				1	2	3
4	5	6	7	8	9	10
11	12	13	14	15	16	17
18	19	20	21	22	23	24
25	26	27	28	29	30	

SCHOOL *Holidays*

AUGUST

SEPTEMBER

OCTOBER

NOVEMBER

DECEMBER

NOTES

SCHOOL *Holidays*

JANUARY

FEBRUARY

MARCH

APRIL

MAY

JUNE

NOTES:

YEAR AT A *Glance*

AUGUST

SEPTEMBER

OCTOBER

NOVEMBER

DECEMBER

JANUARY

FEBRUARY

MARCH

APRIL

MAY

JUNE

NOTES:

STUDENT *Birthdays*

AUGUST

SEPTEMBER

OCTOBER

NOVEMBER

DECEMBER

JANUARY

FEBRUARY

MARCH

APRIL

MAY

JUNE

CLASSROOM *Expenses*

MONTH: **YEAR:**

CLASS:

DATE	ITEM	DESCRIPTION	CATEGORY	COST

DATE:

CLASS *Field Trip*

EVENT

DATE:

LOCATION

TIME

DEPT TIME:

TOTAL COST:

RETURN TIME:

CONTACT

FIELD TRIP *Checklist*

- [ ]   [ ]
- [ ]   [ ]
- [ ]   [ ]
- [ ]   [ ]
- [ ]   [ ]
- [ ]   [ ]
- [ ]   [ ]
- [ ]   [ ]
- [ ]   [ ]
- [ ]   [ ]

IMPORTANT *Reminders*

Field Trip Itinerary

TIME:	ACTIVITIES:

PROGRESS *Report*

CLASS/SUBJECT:

DATE	SUBJECT/CLASS	LESSON PLAN #	ASSIGNMENTS

NOTES & IDEAS   **ASSESSMENT**

CUSTOMIZED ACTION PLAN

ASSIGNMENT *Tracker*

CLASS/SUBJECT: _____   WEEK OF: _____

MONDAY:	TUESDAY	WEDNESDAY

THURSDAY	FRIDAY	NOTES:

READING *Tracker*

CLASS:

BOOK TITLE: AUTHOR:

DATE	STUDENT	PAGES READ	NOTES

MONTHLY *Notes*

AUGUST				
M	T	W	T	F

NOTES, ACTIVITIES, PLANS & IDEAS

MONTHLY *Schedule*

CLASSROOM: **MONTH:**

M	T	W	T	F	S	S

NOTES, ACTIVITIES, PLANS & IDEAS

MONTHLY *Notes*

SEPTEMBER				
M	T	W	T	F

NOTES, ACTIVITIES, PLANS & IDEAS

MONTHLY *Schedule*

CLASSROOM: **MONTH:**

M	T	W	T	F	S	S

NOTES, ACTIVITIES, PLANS & IDEAS

MONTHLY *Notes*

OCTOBER				
M	T	W	T	F

NOTES, ACTIVITIES, PLANS & IDEAS

MONTHLY *Schedule*

CLASSROOM: **MONTH:**

M	T	W	T	F	S	S

NOTES, ACTIVITIES, PLANS & IDEAS

MONTHLY *Notes*

NOVEMBER				
M	T	W	T	F

NOTES, ACTIVITIES, PLANS & IDEAS

MONTHLY *Schedule*

CLASSROOM: **MONTH:**

M	T	W	T	F	S	S

NOTES, ACTIVITIES, PLANS & IDEAS

MONTHLY *Notes*

DECEMBER				
M	T	W	T	F

NOTES, ACTIVITIES, PLANS & IDEAS

MONTHLY *Schedule*

CLASSROOM: **MONTH:**

M	T	W	T	F	S	S

NOTES, ACTIVITIES, PLANS & IDEAS

MONTHLY *Notes*

JANUARY

M	T	W	T	F

NOTES, ACTIVITIES, PLANS & IDEAS

MONTHLY Schedule

CLASSROOM: **MONTH:**

M	T	W	T	F	S	S

NOTES, ACTIVITIES, PLANS & IDEAS

MONTHLY Notes

FEBRUARY				
M	T	W	T	F

NOTES, ACTIVITIES, PLANS & IDEAS

MONTHLY Schedule

CLASSROOM:　　　　　　　　**MONTH:**

M	T	W	T	F	S	S

NOTES, ACTIVITIES, PLANS & IDEAS

MONTHLY Notes

MARCH				
M	T	W	T	F

NOTES, ACTIVITIES, PLANS & IDEAS

MONTHLY Schedule

CLASSROOM: **MONTH:**

M	T	W	T	F	S	S

NOTES, ACTIVITIES, PLANS & IDEAS

MONTHLY Notes

	APRIL			
M	T	W	T	F

NOTES, ACTIVITIES, PLANS & IDEAS

MONTHLY *Schedule*

CLASSROOM: **MONTH:**

M	T	W	T	F	S	S

NOTES, ACTIVITIES, PLANS & IDEAS

MONTHLY *Notes*

	MAY			
M	T	W	T	F

NOTES, ACTIVITIES, PLANS & IDEAS

MONTHLY *Schedule*

CLASSROOM: **MONTH:**

M	T	W	T	F	S	S

NOTES, ACTIVITIES, PLANS & IDEAS

MONTHLY *Notes*

JUNE				
M	T	W	T	F

NOTES, ACTIVITIES, PLANS & IDEAS

MONTHLY *Schedule*

CLASSROOM: **MONTH:**

M	T	W	T	F	S	S

NOTES, ACTIVITIES, PLANS & IDEAS

DATE:

WEEKLY ROLL *Call*

| FIRST NAME: | LAST NAME: | STATUS: |

WEEKLY *Overview*

WEEK OF: ....

MONDAY

TUESDAY

WEDNESDAY

THURSDAY

FRIDAY

SATURDAY

SUNDAY

IMPORTANT NOTES

WEEKLY *Lesson Plan*

MONDAY

EQ/ I CAN NOTES:

TUESDAY

EQ/ I CAN NOTES:

WEDNESDAY

EQ/ I CAN NOTES:

THURSDAY

EQ/ I CAN NOTES:

FRIDAY

EQ/ I CAN NOTES:

CLASS *Projects*

PROJECT TITLE: **DETAILS:**

START DATE: **DUE DATE:**

DATE   **TASK COMPLETED**

READING *Tracker*

CLASS:

BOOK TITLE:		AUTHOR:	
DATE	STUDENT	PAGES READ	NOTES

WEEKLY *Planner*

MONDAY

TUESDAY

WEDNESDAY

THURSDAY

FRIDAY

EQ/I CAN NOTES:

LESSON *Planner*

SUBJECT:

UNIT:

LESSON:

DATE:

OBJECTIVE:

OVERVIEW

TOPICS COVERED

ASSIGNMENTS

NOTES

ASSIGNMENT *Tracker*

CLASS/SUBJECT: _____   WEEK OF: _____

MONDAY: TUESDAY   WEDNESDAY

THURSDAY   FRIDAY   NOTES:

DAILY Schedule

TO DO LIST:

DATE _____

6 AM

7 AM

8 AM

9 AM

10 AM

11 AM

12 PM

1 PM

2 PM

3 PM

4 PM

5 PM

REMINDERS:

6 PM

7 PM

8 PM

NOTES:

9 PM

10 PM

NOTES

DAY PLANNER *Monday*

DATE:

5am:

6am:

7am:

8am:

9am:

10am:

11am:

12pm:

1pm:

2pm:

3pm:

4pm:

DAILY TO DO LIST:

DAILY GOALS:

NOTES & REMINDERS:

DAY PLANNER

DATE:

5am:

6am:

7am:

8am:

9am:

10am:

11am:

12pm:

1pm:

2pm:

3pm:

4pm:

DAILY TO DO LIST:

DAILY GOALS:

NOTES & REMINDERS:

DAY PLANNER *Wednesday*

DATE:

DAILY TO DO LIST:

5am:

6am:

7am:

8am: **DAILY GOALS:**

9am:

10am:

11am:

NOTES & REMINDERS:

12pm:

1pm:

2pm:

3pm:

4pm:

DAY PLANNER *Thursday*

DATE:

5am:

6am:

7am:

8am:

9am:

10am:

11am:

12pm:

1pm:

2pm:

3pm:

4pm:

DAILY TO DO LIST:

DAILY GOALS:

NOTES & REMINDERS:

DAY PLANNER

DATE:

DAILY TO DO LIST:

5am:

6am:

7am:

8am:
                                    DAILY GOALS:

9am:

10am:

11am:
                                    NOTES & REMINDERS:

12pm:

1pm:

2pm:

3pm:

4pm:

DATE:

WEEKLY ROLL *Call*

FIRST NAME: LAST NAME: STATUS:

WEEKLY *Overview*

WEEK OF: ....

MONDAY   **TUESDAY**   **WEDNESDAY**

THURSDAY   **FRIDAY**   **SATURDAY**

SUNDAY

IMPORTANT NOTES

WEEKLY *Lesson Plan*

MONDAY

EQ/ I CAN NOTES:

TUESDAY

EQ/ I CAN NOTES:

WEDNESDAY

EQ/ I CAN NOTES:

THURSDAY

EQ/ I CAN NOTES:

FRIDAY

EQ/ I CAN NOTES:

CLASS *Projects*

PROJECT TITLE: **DETAILS:**

START DATE: **DUE DATE:**

DATE   **TASK COMPLETED**

READING *Tracker*

CLASS:

BOOK TITLE: AUTHOR:

DATE	STUDENT	PAGES READ	NOTES

WEEKLY *Planner*

MONDAY

TUESDAY

WEDNESDAY

THURSDAY

FRIDAY

EQ/I CAN NOTES:

LESSON *Planner*

SUBJECT:

UNIT:

LESSON:

DATE:

OBJECTIVE:

OVERVIEW

TOPICS COVERED

ASSIGNMENTS

NOTES

ASSIGNMENT *Tracker*

CLASS/SUBJECT: _____   WEEK OF: _____

MONDAY: | TUESDAY | WEDNESDAY

THURSDAY | FRIDAY | NOTES:

DAILY *Schedule*

TO DO LIST:

DATE

6 AM

7 AM

8 AM

9 AM

10 AM

11 AM

12 PM

1 PM

2 PM

3 PM

4 PM

5 PM

REMINDERS:

6 PM

7 PM

8 PM

NOTES:

9 PM

10 PM

NOTES

DAY PLANNER *Monday*

DATE:

DAILY TO DO LIST:

5am:

6am:

7am:

8am: **DAILY GOALS:**

9am:

10am:

11am:

                                         NOTES & REMINDERS:

12pm:

1pm:

2pm:

3pm:

4pm:

DAY PLANNER

DATE:

DAILY TO DO LIST:

5am:

6am:

7am:

8am:

DAILY GOALS:

9am:

10am:

11am:

NOTES & REMINDERS:

12pm:

1pm:

2pm:

3pm:

4pm:

DAY PLANNER *Wednesday*

DATE:

DAILY TO DO LIST:

5am:

6am:

7am:

8am: **DAILY GOALS:**

9am:

10am:

11am:

                                            NOTES & REMINDERS:

12pm:

1pm:

2pm:

3pm:

4pm:

DAY PLANNER *Thursday*

DATE:

5am:

6am:

7am:

8am:

9am:

10am:

11am:

12pm:

1pm:

2pm:

3pm:

4pm:

DAILY TO DO LIST:

DAILY GOALS:

NOTES & REMINDERS:

DAY PLANNER

DATE: **DAILY TO DO LIST:**

5am:

6am:

7am:

8am: **DAILY GOALS:**

9am:

10am:

11am:

                                                   NOTES & REMINDERS:

12pm:

1pm:

2pm:

3pm:

4pm:

DATE:

WEEKLY ROLL *Call*

FIRST NAME: LAST NAME: STATUS:

WEEKLY *Overview*

MONDAY

TUESDAY

WEDNESDAY

THURSDAY

FRIDAY

SATURDAY

SUNDAY

IMPORTANT NOTES

WEEKLY *Lesson Plan*

MONDAY

EQ/ I CAN NOTES:

TUESDAY

EQ/ I CAN NOTES:

WEDNESDAY

EQ/ I CAN NOTES:

THURSDAY

EQ/ I CAN NOTES:

FRIDAY

EQ/ I CAN NOTES:

CLASS Projects

PROJECT TITLE: **DETAILS:**

START DATE: **DUE DATE:**

DATE   **TASK COMPLETED**

READING *Tracker*

CLASS:

BOOK TITLE:		AUTHOR:	
DATE	STUDENT	PAGES READ	NOTES

WEEKLY *Planner*

MONDAY

TUESDAY

WEDNESDAY

THURSDAY

FRIDAY

EQ/I CAN NOTES:

LESSON *Planner*

SUBJECT:

UNIT:

LESSON:

DATE:

OBJECTIVE:

OVERVIEW

TOPICS COVERED

ASSIGNMENTS

NOTES

ASSIGNMENT *Tracker*

CLASS/SUBJECT: _____   WEEK OF: _____

MONDAY: TUESDAY   WEDNESDAY

THURSDAY   FRIDAY   NOTES:

DAILY *Schedule*

TO DO LIST:　　　　　　　　**DATE**

REMINDERS:

NOTES:

6 AM

7 AM

8 AM

9 AM

10 AM

11 AM

12 PM

1 PM

2 PM

3 PM

4 PM

5 PM

6 PM

7 PM

8 PM

9 PM

10 PM

NOTES

DAY PLANNER *Monday*

DATE:

DAILY TO DO LIST:

5am:

6am:

7am:

8am:
                                            DAILY GOALS:

9am:

10am:

11am:

NOTES & REMINDERS:

12pm:

1pm:

2pm:

3pm:

4pm:

DAY PLANNER

DATE:

DAILY TO DO LIST:

5am:

6am:

7am:

8am:

DAILY GOALS:

9am:

10am:

11am:

NOTES & REMINDERS:

12pm:

1pm:

2pm:

3pm:

4pm:

DAY PLANNER *Wednesday*

DATE:

5am:

6am:

7am:

8am:

9am:

10am:

11am:

12pm:

1pm:

2pm:

3pm:

4pm:

DAILY TO DO LIST:

DAILY GOALS:

NOTES & REMINDERS:

DAY PLANNER *Thursday*

DATE:

5am:

6am:

7am:

8am:

9am:

10am:

11am:

12pm:

1pm:

2pm:

3pm:

4pm:

DAILY TO DO LIST:

DAILY GOALS:

NOTES & REMINDERS:

DAY PLANNER

DATE:

5am:

6am:

7am:

8am:

9am:

10am:

11am:

12pm:

1pm:

2pm:

3pm:

4pm:

DAILY TO DO LIST:

DAILY GOALS:

NOTES & REMINDERS:

DATE:

WEEKLY ROLL *Call*

FIRST NAME: LAST NAME: STATUS:

WEEKLY *Overview*

WEEK OF: ....

MONDAY   **TUESDAY**   **WEDNESDAY**

THURSDAY   **FRIDAY**   **SATURDAY**

SUNDAY   **IMPORTANT NOTES**

WEEKLY *Lesson Plan*

MONDAY

EQ/ I CAN NOTES:

TUESDAY

EQ/ I CAN NOTES:

WEDNESDAY

EQ/ I CAN NOTES:

THURSDAY

EQ/ I CAN NOTES:

FRIDAY

EQ/ I CAN NOTES:

CLASS *Projects*

PROJECT TITLE: **DETAILS:**

START DATE: **DUE DATE:**

DATE   **TASK COMPLETED**

PROGRESS *Report*

CLASS/SUBJECT:

DATE	SUBJECT/CLASS	LESSON PLAN #	ASSIGNMENTS

NOTES & IDEAS

ASSESSMENT

CUSTOMIZED ACTION PLAN

READING Tracker

CLASS:

BOOK TITLE: **AUTHOR:**

DATE	STUDENT	PAGES READ	NOTES

WEEKLY *Planner*

MONDAY

TUESDAY

WEDNESDAY

THURSDAY

FRIDAY

EQ/I CAN NOTES:

LESSON *Planner*

SUBJECT:

DATE:

UNIT:

OBJECTIVE:

LESSON:

OVERVIEW

TOPICS COVERED

ASSIGNMENTS

NOTES

ASSIGNMENT *Tracker*

CLASS/SUBJECT: _____   WEEK OF: _____

MONDAY:	TUESDAY	WEDNESDAY

THURSDAY	FRIDAY	NOTES:

DAILY *Schedule*

TO DO LIST: **DATE**

6 AM

7 AM

8 AM

9 AM

10 AM

11 AM

12 PM

1 PM

2 PM

3 PM

4 PM

5 PM

REMINDERS:

6 PM

7 PM

8 PM

NOTES:

9 PM

10 PM

NOTES

DAY PLANNER *Monday*

DATE: _____

5am:

6am:

7am:

8am:

9am:

10am:

11am:

12pm:

1pm:

2pm:

3pm:

4pm:

DAILY TO DO LIST:

DAILY GOALS:

NOTES & REMINDERS:

DAY PLANNER

DATE:

DAILY TO DO LIST:

5am:

6am:

7am:

8am: **DAILY GOALS:**

9am:

10am:

11am:

                                        NOTES & REMINDERS:
12pm:

1pm:

2pm:

3pm:

4pm:

DAY PLANNER *Wednesday*

DATE:

DAILY TO DO LIST:

5am:

6am:

7am:

8am:

DAILY GOALS:

9am:

10am:

11am:

NOTES & REMINDERS:

12pm:

1pm:

2pm:

3pm:

4pm:

DAY PLANNER *Thursday*

DATE:

DAILY TO DO LIST:

5am:

6am:

7am:

8am: **DAILY GOALS:**

9am:

10am:

11am:

                                          NOTES & REMINDERS:

12pm:

1pm:

2pm:

3pm:

4pm:

DAY PLANNER  Friday

DATE:

5am:

6am:

7am:

8am:

9am:

10am:

11am:

12pm:

1pm:

2pm:

3pm:

4pm:

DAILY TO DO LIST:

DAILY GOALS:

NOTES & REMINDERS:

DATE:

WEEKLY ROLL *Call*

FIRST NAME: LAST NAME: STATUS:

WEEKLY *Overview*

WEEK OF: ....

MONDAY

TUESDAY

WEDNESDAY

THURSDAY

FRIDAY

SATURDAY

SUNDAY

IMPORTANT NOTES

WEEKLY *Lesson Plan*

MONDAY

EQ/ I CAN NOTES:

TUESDAY

EQ/ I CAN NOTES:

WEDNESDAY

EQ/ I CAN NOTES:

THURSDAY

EQ/ I CAN NOTES:

FRIDAY

EQ/ I CAN NOTES:

CLASS Projects

PROJECT TITLE: **DETAILS:**

START DATE: **DUE DATE:**

DATE	TASK COMPLETED

READING *Tracker*

CLASS:

BOOK TITLE: AUTHOR:

DATE	STUDENT	PAGES READ	NOTES

WEEKLY *Planner*

MONDAY

TUESDAY

WEDNESDAY

THURSDAY

FRIDAY

EQ/I CAN NOTES:

LESSON *Planner*

SUBJECT:

UNIT:

LESSON:

DATE:

OBJECTIVE:

OVERVIEW

TOPICS COVERED

ASSIGNMENTS

NOTES

ASSIGNMENT *Tracker*

CLASS/SUBJECT: ———————————————— WEEK OF: ————————————————

MONDAY:	TUESDAY	WEDNESDAY

THURSDAY	FRIDAY	NOTES:

DAILY Schedule

TO DO LIST:

DATE

6 AM

7 AM

8 AM

9 AM

10 AM

11 AM

12 PM

1 PM

2 PM

3 PM

4 PM

5 PM

REMINDERS:

6 PM

7 PM

8 PM

9 PM

NOTES:

10 PM

NOTES

DAY PLANNER *Monday*

DATE:

5am:

6am:

7am:

8am:

9am:

10am:

11am:

12pm:

1pm:

2pm:

3pm:

4pm:

DAILY TO DO LIST:

DAILY GOALS:

NOTES & REMINDERS:

DAY PLANNER

DATE:

DAILY TO DO LIST:

5am:

6am:

7am:

8am:

DAILY GOALS:

9am:

10am:

11am:

NOTES & REMINDERS:

12pm:

1pm:

2pm:

3pm:

4pm:

DAY PLANNER *Wednesday*

DATE: **DAILY TO DO LIST:**

5am:

6am:

7am:

8am: **DAILY GOALS:**

9am:

10am:

11am:

                                             NOTES & REMINDERS:

12pm:

1pm:

2pm:

3pm:

4pm:

DAY PLANNER *Thursday*

DATE: **DAILY TO DO LIST:**

5am:

6am:

7am:

8am: **DAILY GOALS:**

9am:

10am:

11am:

                                             NOTES & REMINDERS:

12pm:

1pm:

2pm:

3pm:

4pm:

DAY PLANNER *Friday*

DATE:

5am:

6am:

7am:

8am:

9am:

10am:

11am:

12pm:

1pm:

2pm:

3pm:

4pm:

DAILY TO DO LIST:

DAILY GOALS:

NOTES & REMINDERS:

DATE:

WEEKLY ROLL *Call*

FIRST NAME: LAST NAME: STATUS:

WEEKLY *Overview*

WEEK OF: ....

MONDAY

TUESDAY

WEDNESDAY

THURSDAY

FRIDAY

SATURDAY

SUNDAY

IMPORTANT NOTES

WEEKLY *Lesson Plan*

MONDAY

EQ/ I CAN NOTES:

TUESDAY

EQ/ I CAN NOTES:

WEDNESDAY

EQ/ I CAN NOTES:

THURSDAY

EQ/ I CAN NOTES:

FRIDAY

EQ/ I CAN NOTES:

CLASS Projects

PROJECT TITLE: **DETAILS:**

START DATE: **DUE DATE:**

DATE	TASK COMPLETED

READING *Tracker*

CLASS:

BOOK TITLE: AUTHOR:

DATE	STUDENT	PAGES READ	NOTES

WEEKLY *Planner*

MONDAY

TUESDAY

WEDNESDAY

THURSDAY

FRIDAY

EQ/I CAN NOTES:

LESSON *Planner*

SUBJECT:

UNIT:

LESSON:

DATE:

OBJECTIVE:

OVERVIEW

TOPICS COVERED

ASSIGNMENTS

NOTES

ASSIGNMENT *Tracker*

CLASS/SUBJECT: _____   WEEK OF: _____

MONDAY:	TUESDAY	WEDNESDAY

THURSDAY	FRIDAY	NOTES:

DAILY Schedule

TO DO LIST:

DATE

6 AM

7 AM

8 AM

9 AM

10 AM

11 AM

12 PM

1 PM

2 PM

3 PM

4 PM

5 PM

REMINDERS:

6 PM

7 PM

8 PM

9 PM

NOTES:

10 PM

NOTES

DAY PLANNER *Monday*

DATE:

5am:

6am:

7am:

8am:

9am:

10am:

11am:

12pm:

1pm:

2pm:

3pm:

4pm:

DAILY TO DO LIST:

DAILY GOALS:

NOTES & REMINDERS:

DAY PLANNER

DATE:

DAILY TO DO LIST:

5am:

6am:

7am:

8am: **DAILY GOALS:**

9am:

10am:

11am:

                                        NOTES & REMINDERS:

12pm:

1pm:

2pm:

3pm:

4pm:

DAY PLANNER *Wednesday*

DATE:

5am:

6am:

7am:

8am:

9am:

10am:

11am:

12pm:

1pm:

2pm:

3pm:

4pm:

DAILY TO DO LIST:

DAILY GOALS:

NOTES & REMINDERS:

DAY PLANNER *Thursday*

DATE:

DAILY TO DO LIST:

5am:

6am:

7am:

8am: **DAILY GOALS:**

9am:

10am:

11am:

NOTES & REMINDERS:

12pm:

1pm:

2pm:

3pm:

4pm:

DAY PLANNER

DATE:

5am:

6am:

7am:

8am:

9am:

10am:

11am:

12pm:

1pm:

2pm:

3pm:

4pm:

DAILY TO DO LIST:

DAILY GOALS:

NOTES & REMINDERS:

DATE:

WEEKLY ROLL *Call*

| FIRST NAME: | LAST NAME: | STATUS: |

WEEKLY *Overview*

WEEK OF: ....

MONDAY   **TUESDAY**   **WEDNESDAY**

THURSDAY   **FRIDAY**   **SATURDAY**

SUNDAY   **IMPORTANT NOTES**

WEEKLY *Lesson Plan*

MONDAY

EQ/ I CAN NOTES:

TUESDAY

EQ/ I CAN NOTES:

WEDNESDAY

EQ/ I CAN NOTES:

THURSDAY

EQ/ I CAN NOTES:

FRIDAY

EQ/ I CAN NOTES:

READING *Tracker*

CLASS:

BOOK TITLE: AUTHOR:

DATE	STUDENT	PAGES READ	NOTES

LESSON *Planner*

SUBJECT:

DATE:

UNIT:

OBJECTIVE:

LESSON:

OVERVIEW

TOPICS COVERED

ASSIGNMENTS

NOTES

ASSIGNMENT *Tracker*

CLASS/SUBJECT: _____   WEEK OF: _____

MONDAY:	TUESDAY	WEDNESDAY

THURSDAY	FRIDAY	NOTES:

DAY PLANNER *Monday*

DATE:

5am:

6am:

7am:

8am:

9am:

10am:

11am:

12pm:

1pm:

2pm:

3pm:

4pm:

DAILY TO DO LIST:

DAILY GOALS:

NOTES & REMINDERS:

DAY PLANNER

DATE:

5am:

6am:

7am:

8am:

9am:

10am:

11am:

12pm:

1pm:

2pm:

3pm:

4pm:

DAILY TO DO LIST:

DAILY GOALS:

NOTES & REMINDERS:

DAY PLANNER *Wednesday*

DATE:

5am:

6am:

7am:

8am:

9am:

10am:

11am:

12pm:

1pm:

2pm:

3pm:

4pm:

DAILY TO DO LIST:

DAILY GOALS:

NOTES & REMINDERS:

DAY PLANNER *Thursday*

DATE:

5am:

6am:

7am:

8am:

9am:

10am:

11am:

12pm:

1pm:

2pm:

3pm:

4pm:

DAILY TO DO LIST:

DAILY GOALS:

NOTES & REMINDERS:

DAY PLANNER

DATE:

DAILY TO DO LIST:

5am:

6am:

7am:

8am: **DAILY GOALS:**

9am:

10am:

11am:

                                            NOTES & REMINDERS:

12pm:

1pm:

2pm:

3pm:

4pm:

DATE: _____

WEEKLY ROLL *Call*

| FIRST NAME: | LAST NAME: | STATUS: |

WEEKLY *Overview*

WEEK OF: ....

MONDAY

TUESDAY

WEDNESDAY

THURSDAY

FRIDAY

SATURDAY

SUNDAY

IMPORTANT NOTES

WEEKLY *Lesson Plan*

MONDAY

EQ/ I CAN NOTES:

TUESDAY

EQ/ I CAN NOTES:

WEDNESDAY

EQ/ I CAN NOTES:

THURSDAY

EQ/ I CAN NOTES:

FRIDAY

EQ/ I CAN NOTES:

LESSON *Planner*

SUBJECT:

UNIT:

LESSON:

DATE:

OBJECTIVE:

OVERVIEW

TOPICS COVERED

ASSIGNMENTS

NOTES

READING Tracker

CLASS:

BOOK TITLE: AUTHOR:

DATE	STUDENT	PAGES READ	NOTES

DAY PLANNER *Monday*

DATE:

5am:

6am:

7am:

8am:

9am:

10am:

11am:

12pm:

1pm:

2pm:

3pm:

4pm:

DAILY TO DO LIST:

DAILY GOALS:

NOTES & REMINDERS:

DAY PLANNER

DATE:

DAILY TO DO LIST:

5am:

6am:

7am:

8am: **DAILY GOALS:**

9am:

10am:

11am:

                                                           NOTES & REMINDERS:

12pm:

1pm:

2pm:

3pm:

4pm:

DAY PLANNER *Wednesday*

DATE:

5am:

6am:

7am:

8am:

9am:

10am:

11am:

12pm:

1pm:

2pm:

3pm:

4pm:

DAILY TO DO LIST:

DAILY GOALS:

NOTES & REMINDERS:

DAY PLANNER *Thursday*

DATE:

DAILY TO DO LIST:

5am:

6am:

7am:

8am: **DAILY GOALS:**

9am:

10am:

11am:
                                              NOTES & REMINDERS:
12pm:

1pm:

2pm:

3pm:

4pm:

DAY PLANNER

DATE:

5am:

6am:

7am:

8am:

9am:

10am:

11am:

12pm:

1pm:

2pm:

3pm:

4pm:

DAILY TO DO LIST:

DAILY GOALS:

NOTES & REMINDERS:

STUDENT *Information*

STUDENT INFORMATION

NAME: BIRTH DATE:

ADDRESS: PARENTS NAMES:

PHONE: EMAIL ADDRESS:

ACADEMIC HISTORY   ### MEDICAL INFORMATION

STUDENT ID:

CHALLENGES:

STRENGTHS:

PRIMARY CONTACT INFORMATION   ### EMERGENCY CONTACT INFORMATION

ADDITIONAL INFORMATION

STUDENT *Information*

STUDENT INFORMATION

NAME: BIRTH DATE:

ADDRESS: PARENTS NAMES:

PHONE: EMAIL ADDRESS:

ACADEMIC HISTORY   ### MEDICAL INFORMATION

STUDENT ID:

CHALLENGES:

STRENGTHS:

PRIMARY CONTACT INFORMATION   ### EMERGENCY CONTACT INFORMATION

ADDITIONAL INFORMATION

STUDENT *Information*

STUDENT INFORMATION

NAME: _____

ADDRESS: _____

PHONE: _____

BIRTH DATE: _____

PARENTS NAMES: _____

EMAIL ADDRESS: _____

ACADEMIC HISTORY

STUDENT ID: _____

CHALLENGES: _____

STRENGTHS: _____

MEDICAL INFORMATION

PRIMARY CONTACT INFORMATION

EMERGENCY CONTACT INFORMATION

ADDITIONAL INFORMATION

PARENT-TEACHER *Meetings*

STUDENT NAME:

DATE & TIME:

REASON FOR MEETING

TOPICS DISCUSSED

ACTION PLAN & GOALS

STUDENT NAME:

DATE & TIME:

REASON FOR MEETING

TOPICS DISCUSSED

ACTION PLAN & GOALS

PARENT-TEACHER *Meetings*

STUDENT NAME:

DATE & TIME:

REASON FOR MEETING

TOPICS DISCUSSED

ACTION PLAN & GOALS

STUDENT NAME:

DATE & TIME:

REASON FOR MEETING

TOPICS DISCUSSED

ACTION PLAN & GOALS

PARENT-TEACHER *Meetings*

STUDENT NAME:

DATE & TIME:

REASON FOR MEETING

TOPICS DISCUSSED

ACTION PLAN & GOALS

STUDENT NAME:

DATE & TIME:

REASON FOR MEETING

TOPICS DISCUSSED

ACTION PLAN & GOALS

PARENT *Contacts*

STUDENT:

PARENTS:

PHONE #:

EMAIL:

STUDENT:

PARENTS:

PHONE #:

EMAIL:

STUDENT:

PARENTS:

PHONE #:

EMAIL:

STUDENT:

PARENTS:

PHONE #:

EMAIL:

STUDENT:

PARENTS:

PHONE #:

EMAIL:

STUDENT:

PARENTS:

PHONE #:

EMAIL:

STUDENT:

PARENTS:

PHONE #:

EMAIL:

STUDENT:

PARENTS:

PHONE #:

EMAIL:

STUDENT:

PARENTS:

PHONE #:

EMAIL:

STUDENT:

PARENTS:

PHONE #:

EMAIL:

PARENT *Contacts*

STUDENT:

PARENTS:

PHONE #:

EMAIL:

STUDENT:

PARENTS:

PHONE #:

EMAIL:

STUDENT:

PARENTS:

PHONE #:

EMAIL:

STUDENT:

PARENTS:

PHONE #:

EMAIL:

STUDENT:

PARENTS:

PHONE #:

EMAIL:

STUDENT:

PARENTS:

PHONE #:

EMAIL:

STUDENT:

PARENTS:

PHONE #:

EMAIL:

STUDENT:

PARENTS:

PHONE #:

EMAIL:

STUDENT:

PARENTS:

PHONE #:

EMAIL:

STUDENT:

PARENTS:

PHONE #:

EMAIL:

PARENT *Contacts*

STUDENT:

PARENTS:

PHONE #:

EMAIL:

STUDENT:

PARENTS:

PHONE #:

EMAIL:

STUDENT:

PARENTS:

PHONE #:

EMAIL:

STUDENT:

PARENTS:

PHONE #:

EMAIL:

STUDENT:

PARENTS:

PHONE #:

EMAIL:

STUDENT:

PARENTS:

PHONE #:

EMAIL:

STUDENT:

PARENTS:

PHONE #:

EMAIL:

STUDENT:

PARENTS:

PHONE #:

EMAIL:

STUDENT:

PARENTS:

PHONE #:

EMAIL:

STUDENT:

PARENTS:

PHONE #:

EMAIL:

PARENT CONTACT *Log*

MONTH:

NAME & DATE:	REASON:	METHOD:	NOTES:
		EMAIL:	
		PHONE:	
		MEETING:	

DATE:	REASON:	METHOD:	NOTES:
		EMAIL:	
		PHONE:	
		MEETING:	

DATE:	REASON:	METHOD:	NOTES:
		EMAIL:	
		PHONE:	
		MEETING:	

DATE:	REASON:	METHOD:	NOTES:
		EMAIL:	
		PHONE:	
		MEETING:	

DATE:	REASON:	METHOD:	NOTES:
		EMAIL:	
		PHONE:	
		MEETING:	

NOTES

PARENT CONTACT *Log*

MONTH:

NAME & DATE:	REASON:	METHOD:	NOTES:
		EMAIL:	
		PHONE:	
		MEETING:	

DATE:	REASON:	METHOD:	NOTES:
		EMAIL:	
		PHONE:	
		MEETING:	

DATE:	REASON:	METHOD:	NOTES:
		EMAIL:	
		PHONE:	
		MEETING:	

DATE:	REASON:	METHOD:	NOTES:
		EMAIL:	
		PHONE:	
		MEETING:	

DATE:	REASON:	METHOD:	NOTES:
		EMAIL:	
		PHONE:	
		MEETING:	

NOTES

Made in the USA
Monee, IL
31 July 2022